Interactive White Activities for Music

35 ready-to-use activities on CD-ROM

Steve Block and Andy Murray

**Badger
Publishing**

INTRODUCTION

The growth in use of interactive whiteboards in UK schools over the past few years has been rapid, to say the least.

When used well, the interactive whiteboard (IWB) can transform and revitalise teaching and learning in any subject and at any level. The IWB can help to engage and motivate students, focus their learning and provide an invaluable central resource base in the classroom – and all at the touch of a pen or a finger.

Many secondary music departments now have, or expect soon to have, an IWB in their teaching area. However, the publication of subject-specific music activities has so far been minimal in comparison to most other curriculum areas. Whilst the various software packages accompanying IWBs normally allow teachers to create their own resources and activities, this can be time-consuming and require no small level of skill and experience for anything at all sophisticated in design.

This product has therefore been produced to help meet this substantial need in secondary music departments.

The scope of the activities

The CD-ROM accompanying this Teacher Book contains six main types of activity. One of these has ten variants and the other five have five variants, thus providing 35 activities in all. Teachers already familiar with the *Badger Key Stage 3 Music Starters* (2004) will recognise that several of the activity types and their contents have been adapted for the IWB from that publication.

As can be seen from the learning objectives for each activity type, these activities call upon students' ability to demonstrate skills in **performing**, **music reading** and **listening**, as well as recalling and applying musical **knowledge and understanding**. A glance at the charts and lists at the back of this book will quickly demonstrate the wide range of content in these activities.

Each of the activities has built into it a degree of flexibility that allows different approaches in delivery, thus allowing teachers to adapt any activity to the teaching and learning environment in which it is to be used. Furthermore, there are varying degrees of progression built into both content and delivery options for all of the activities, making them suitable for use at any point in KS3 or indeed in KS4.

The activities could be used at any point in a lesson, for example:
- as **starters** to engage and motivate students at the beginning of the lesson, or to review and consolidate work from the previous lesson;
- as **'breathing points'** part-way through a longer lesson, in 'brain gym' style;
- as **plenaries** to review and consolidate learning from the current lesson;
- as **assessment** opportunities, through observing individuals and whole classes engaged in a range of challenges, e.g. in practical and listening skills and in knowledge and understanding.

Using the activities in the classroom

These activities are designed to make use of the **interactive** possibilities of the IWB, and not just to replace the writing on the whiteboard with something colourful for students to look at while the teacher talks and points! In other words, students should be engaged either as individuals making decisions at the whiteboard itself, or by responding to the activity requirements from their seats as a whole class or in groups. In the latter case, either the teacher or a student can operate the activity screen on behalf of the class.

Because the activity screens require clicks or drags of the pen/finger on the appropriate button or box, it is vital that your IWB is correctly set up and accurately oriented/calibrated beforehand. There is nothing more frustrating for teacher and students than trying to click on a button on the screen, only to find that the cursor appears several inches away from the tip of your pen or finger!

It is also crucial with most of the activities to have space on either side of the IWB for you or one of your students (two students, in the case of *Don't Panic!*) to stand and operate the board without obscuring the screen for the rest of the class.

Every activity is supported in this Teacher Book by detailed guidance and labelled screenshots. However, there can be no substitute for simply trying out the activities for yourself (even if only with the mouse on your computer at home) and practising a little with them, so that there are no awkward moments where you are not sure what to do next.

Remember that where knowledge and understanding are a key element of the activity, not every word, term or concept will be known by every student in the class - indeed there may be areas that the class have not yet covered. However, the activities can be used as much for developing knowledge as for recalling it, and a degree of timely support from you can create some valuable learning opportunities. If you do need to check what vocabulary or concepts are contained in any activity, just consult the charts and lists at the back of the book.

Technical information

There are 35 activities in all. Five of them are PowerPoint files, which require that users already have Microsoft's PowerPoint program (available for Windows and Mac). The remaining 30 activities are stand-alone program files, requiring no additional software. All 30 are versioned for both Windows and Mac computers on the CD-ROM. Users need to have a web browser in order to access the CD-ROM menu, but it is not necessary to have an internet connection. Further information is given in the help files on the CD-ROM.

The five variants of *Flash Card Rhythms* are in "PowerPoint Show" (.pps) format on the CD-ROM. **These files should be opened directly from the folder in which they are located (on the CD-ROM or elsewhere on your computer). They should NOT be opened through the 'Open File' menu within PowerPoint itself**, otherwise the PowerPoint Show format will be lost. If this happens, the pointer will not remain visible throughout the activity and it will not always be easy to make it reappear. The only way to get around this would be to right-click on the screen once the activity is running, go to 'Pointer Options', then 'Arrow Options' and click on 'Visible'. This would need to be done every time an activity is opened and run from within the PowerPoint programme itself.

SOUND AND PICTURE RESOURCES

Activity and variant	Title	Description	
Drag & Drop 1-10	Sound clips	Sound clips created with Magix 'Music Maker' software, Sibelius software (with Garritan 'Personal Orchestra') and Yamaha DGX-205 keyboard, or provided by kind permission of Northumberland County Music Service (from Northumberland NGfL 'Virtual Orchestra'.	
	Images	Harpsichord image: © Michael Boys/CORBIS. All other images from iStock Royalty Free Collection (www.istockphoto.com).	
Mix & Match 1 (Symphony orchestra)	Excerpt A	Sabre Dance	From Khachaturian: "Gayaneh" (St. Petersburg State Symphony Orchestra).
	Excerpt B	Lullaby	
	Excerpt C	Choosing the Bride	
Mix & Match 2 (String quartet)	Excerpt A	Boisterous Bourree	From Britten: String: Simple Symphony (Maggini Quartet).
	Excerpt B	Playful Pizzicato	
	Excerpt C	Sentimental Saraband	
	Excerpt D	Frolicsome Finale	
Mix & Match 3 (Orchestral effects)	Excerpt A	Smooth 'n' spiky	Created by Steve Block using sound samples from Magix 'Music Maker' and by courtesy of the Philharmonia Orchestra. (For more free samples visit www.philharmonia.co.uk/thesoundexchange)
	Excerpt B	Stringy nines	
	Excerpt C	Scary orchestra	
Mix & Match 4 (Various styles)	Excerpt A	The Bonesetter's Dance	Klezmer Café Jew Zoo (Yale Strom)
	Excerpt B	Sensemaya	Revueltas (Mexico Festival Orchestra)
	Excerpt C	2nd movement	Tchaikovsky Symphony No.6 (Polish National Radio Symphony Orchestra)
	Excerpt D	Blues Guaguanco	Cuban Jazz (Alfredo Rodriguez y Los Acereko)
Mix & Match 4 (World music)	Excerpt A	Ndakuvara	The Tuku Years (Oliver Mtukudzi)
	Excerpt B	Bitilé	Ma Ya (Habib Koité)
	Excerpt C	Ambush on all Sides	Pipa Favourites (Liu Dehai)
	Excerpt D	Ludiane Nachdi Nu	Bhangra Beatz (Bhangra Beatz)

CONTENTS

Activity type	Variants
Drag & Drop (page 6)	1. Keyboard instruments 2. Woodwind instruments 3. String instruments 4. Brass instruments 5. Percussion instruments 6. Dynamics 7. Pitch 8. Rhythm & style 9. Texture 10. Tempo
Mix & Match (page 8)	1. Symphony orchestra 2. String quartet 3. Orchestral effects 4. Various styles 5. World music
Predict-ability (page 10)	1. Level 1 2. Level 2 3. Level 3 4. Level 4 5. Level 5
Don't Panic! (page 12)	1. Musical elements 2. Musical instruments 3. Musical genres 4. Classic rock & pop hits 5. Numbers in music
Blob Grid (page 14)	1. 4 x 4 (simple metre, basic) 2. 4 x 4 (simple metre, extended) 3. 5 x 5 (simple metre) 4. 4 x 4 (compound metre) 5. 4 x 4 (graphic symbols)
Flash Card Rhythms (page 16)	1. 4/4 time 2. 3/4 time 3. 5/4 time 4. 6/8 time 5. Graphic symbols
Answers and Notes (page 18)	
Appendices 1 & 2 (page 32)	CD FAQs

Drag and Drop

LEARNING OBJECTIVES

- Comparing and contrasting musical sounds and phrases;
- identifying instrumental timbres;
- developing knowledge and understanding of key terms relating to musical elements.

DESCRIPTION OF ACTIVITY AND VARIANTS

Students must match the sounds in 4 musical excerpts with their corresponding pictures or descriptions. There are 10 variants, each covering a different category:

1.	Keyboard instruments	(pipe organ, synthesiser, piano, harpsichord)
2.	Woodwind instruments	(saxophone, recorder, bass clarinet, bassoon)
3.	String instruments	(cello, acoustic guitar, viola, bass guitar)
4.	Brass instruments	(tuba, bugle, french horn, trombone)
5.	Percussion instruments	(tambourine, djembe, hi-hat cymbal, timpani)
6.	Dynamics	(crescendo, ff / p, diminuendo, pp / mf / ff)
7.	Pitch	(melodic phrases: 2 staff notation, 2 graphic notation)
8.	Rhythm & style	(waltz, reggae, swing, march)
9.	Texture	(melody with chordal accompaniment, round, solo, duet)
10.	Tempo	(presto, accelerando, ritenuto, adagio)

The musical excerpts are drawn from a wide range of musical styles and genres, and are sufficiently differentiated within each category to avoid ambiguity when matching with the pictures or descriptions. The pictures in variants 1-5 often show the instruments being played, but do not always reveal the whole instrument. This provides an extra element of fun and challenge to the activity. Keeping the sound separate from its picture and name supports the objective of identifying instruments by timbre, and focuses on listening skill rather than visual memory.

WAYS OF USING THE ACTIVITY

Drag and Drop can be used to develop and consolidate students' listening skills and understanding of key concepts in an entertaining yet quite intensive manner. The whole activity could be led by the teacher at the whiteboard, guided by students' responses, or individual students could be invited to activate the sounds and/or 'drag and drop' the boxes. In the latter case, the student could be asked to respond on his/her own or on the advice of others in the class (e.g. pairs, groups, teams, whole class).

The musical excerpts can be played in any order, as often as required, partially or completely. Thus the activity becomes far more immediate and interactive than the usual listening exercise.

Since each category is a separate activity, the focus(es) can be selected by the teacher as appropriate to the lesson and the overall activity can be made as short or as long as necessary.

Drag and Drop

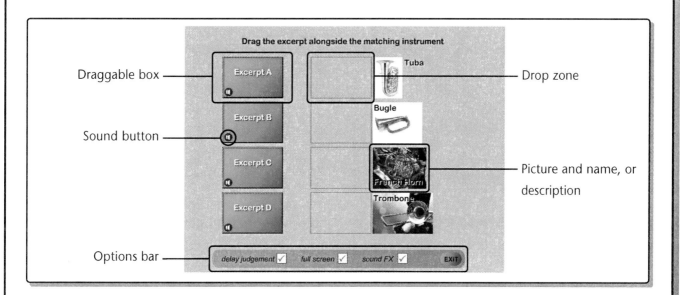

THE ACTIVITY SCREENS

Introductory screens:
These give operational guidance: *"On the next screen there are four musical excerpts. Each excerpt is a short recording of a different (brass, etc) instrument. Drag the excerpt alongside the matching instrument."*

Main screens:
As the main screen appears, the four **draggable boxes** with the **sound buttons** will fly in from the left. Clicking a sound button once will start the excerpt; clicking it again or clicking a different sound button will both stop the current excerpt playing.

Each draggable box must be dragged onto the correct **drop zone**. Draggable boxes cannot be dragged by their sound buttons.

Options bar:
The **delay judgement** option allows you to determine whether the placement of each 'drag and drop' will be judged immediately or delayed until all four have been made. Leaving the box 'checked' prevents students from achieving purely by trial and error. Unchecking the box means that each answer will be tested in turn, allowing another student or team to try an alternative answer. Note that boxes dragged into an incorrect target area will be automatically rejected when the 'judgement' is made.

Unchecking the **full screen** option will allow you to access other windows on the whiteboard, or even to run several different categories of *Drag and Drop* at the same time.

The **sound FX** option allows you to turn off the sound effects that normally accompany correct and incorrect judgements.

The **exit** button closes the activity completely.

Mix and Match

LEARNING OBJECTIVES

- Comparing and contrasting a range of musical excerpts by ear;
- recognising key features relating to style, genre, compositional devices and all musical elements;
- developing knowledge and understanding of key terms and concepts.

DESCRIPTION OF ACTIVITY AND VARIANTS

Students must match various descriptive statements with a number of musical excerpts. There are 5 variants, each covering a different style, genre or set of same:

1. Symphony orchestra   (3 excerpts from Khachaturian's *Gayaneh* suite)
2. String quartet   (4 excerpts from Britten's *Simple Symphony*)
3. Orchestral effects   (3 excerpts with contrasting textures and instrumentation)
4. Various styles   (4 excerpts: European 'classical', Jewish Klezmer, Cuban Jazz, S. American 'classical')
5. World music   (4 excerpts: India, China, Africa/Zimbabwe, Africa/Mali)

Some categories have only a few statements to match, others have multiple statements in sets. Thus the degree of challenge will vary according to the category selected, as well as students' prior musical learning and experience. The recognition and understanding of key vocabulary is a vital aspect of every category. However, *Mix and Match* will provide many opportunities for students to acquire new knowledge and understanding as well as to consolidate their prior learning.

WAYS OF USING THE ACTIVITY

Drag and Drop can be used to develop and consolidate students' listening skills and understanding of key concepts in an entertaining yet quite intensive manner. The whole activity could be led by the teacher at the whiteboard, guided by students' responses, or individual students could be invited to activate the sounds and/or 'drag and drop' the boxes. In the latter case, the student could be asked to respond on his/her own or on the advice of others in the class (e.g. pairs, groups, teams, whole class).

The musical excerpts can be played in any order, as often as required, partially or completely. Thus the activity becomes far more immediate and interactive than the usual listening exercise.

Since each category is a separate activity, the focus(es) can be selected by the teacher as appropriate to the lesson and the overall activity can be made as short or as long as necessary.

ANSWERS FOR ALL VARIANTS OF *MIX AND MATCH*
CAN BE FOUND ON PAGE 18.

Mix and Match

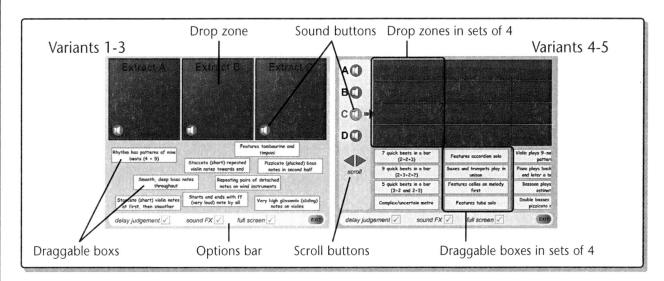

THE ACTIVITY SCREENS

Introductory screens:
These give operational guidance. All variants: *"There are (x) musical excerpts and (y) descriptions."* Variants 1-3 continue: *"Listen to the excerpts and drag each description into the box containing the matching music."* Variants 4-5 continue: *"For each set of descriptions, decide which phrase applies to which excerpt and drag it to the correct line. You can scroll left and right to see any set of descriptions that is out of view."*

Main screen:
In variants 1-3 (see left screenshot), the ***draggable boxes*** may be dragged to any ***drop zone*** and will snap into any position within the chosen box when released. The ***sound buttons*** can be clicked at any time during the activity to start and stop the sound.

In variants 4-5 (see right screenshot), the ***draggable boxes*** and ***drop zones*** are ***in sets in four***. Within any set, each musical feature must be dragged into one of the four drop zones in the same column. Note that the musical features in each column are often related. Because of the number of columns required for variants 4-5, ***scroll buttons*** have been added to scroll left or right across the five columns.

Options bar:
The ***delay judgement*** option allows you to determine whether the placement of each 'drag and drop' will be judged immediately or delayed until all have been made. Leaving the box 'checked' prevents students from achieving purely by trial and error. Unchecking the box means that each answer will be tested in turn, allowing another student or team to try an alternative answer. Note that boxes dragged into an incorrect target area will be automatically rejected when the 'judgement' is made.

Unchecking the ***full screen*** option will allow you to access other windows on the whiteboard, or even to run several different categories of *Drag and Drop* at the same time.

The ***sound FX*** option allows you to turn off the sound effects that normally accompany correct and incorrect judgements. The ***exit*** button closes the activity completely.

Predict-ability

LEARNING OBJECTIVES

- Recalling and applying prior knowledge to predict answers;
- using logic and elimination to sift knowledge;
- developing knowledge and understanding of key musical terms.

DESCRIPTION OF ACTIVITY AND VARIANTS

Students must try to predict answers correctly after receiving 4 increasingly specific clues. There are 5 variants (levels), each containing 10 questions across the following categories:

People   Instruments   Types of music   Musical terms   Pot luck

There is a degree of progression through the 5 levels. Level 1 may be seen as more appropriate to lower KS3 and Level 5 to upper KS3.

The clues and answers are drawn from a range of musical styles and genres.

WAYS OF USING THE ACTIVITY

Predict-ability can be used to develop and consolidate students' knowledge and understanding of key concepts and vocabulary in an entertaining yet quite intensive manner. The whole activity could be led by the teacher at the whiteboard, guided by students' responses or individual students could be invited to activate the clues. In the latter case, the student could be asked to respond on his/her own or on the advice of others in the class (e.g. pairs, groups, teams, whole class).

Each set of clues is framed within a hexagon on the screen. Each time you progress to the next clue, the previous one is added to a list of previous clues for future reference. You could ask students to write down what their current prediction for the answer might be or invite individuals to suggest predictions. As the four clues become progressively more specific, students should be able to hone in on the correct answer. This will engage them in a problem-solving process which will require comparisons, contrasts, eliminations, not to mention frequent changes of mind.

Thus the thinking around one set of clues might go like this:

Clue 2a:	Instrument	**1st prediction/guess:**	Violin?
Clue 2b:	Made of metal	**2nd prediction/guess:**	Trumpet or cymbal?
Clue 2c:	Used in jazz and pop, and sometimes classical	**3rd prediction/guess:**	Still trumpet.
Clue 2d:	Mouthpiece has a single reed	**Final prediction:**	Ah! Saxophone.

The sets of clues can be played in any order, partially or completely. Thus it is possible to have several hexagons open at the same time if desired, giving students the option of continuing with one set, picking up another partially completed set or starting a new set.

**CLUES AND ANSWERS FOR ALL VARIANTS
OF *PREDICT-ABILITY* CAN BE FOUND ON PAGE 20.**

Predict-ability

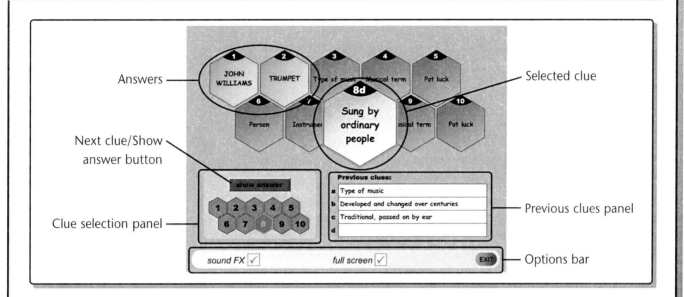

Answers — JOHN WILLIAMS · TRUMPET

Selected clue

8d Sung by ordinary people

Next clue/Show answer button

Clue selection panel

show answer

Previous clues panel

Previous clues:

a	Type of music
b	Developed and changed over centuries
c	Traditional, passed on by ear
d	

sound FX ✓   full screen ✓   EXIT — Options bar

THE ACTIVITY SCREENS

Introductory screens:
These give operational guidance: *"There are 10 sets of clues. In each set there are four clues leading to an answer. The first clue is quite broad. Each successive clue will narrow down the possibilities a little more. The final clue will take you quite close to the answer. How good are you at predicting what that answer might be as the clues are revealed?"*

Main screens:
A particular set of clues can be selected from the **clue selection panel** (but not by clicking the larger hexagons containing text). This will reveal the **selected clue** magnified and highlighted above.

Click the **'show next clue'** button to progress through the clues. Previous clues are logged in the **'previous clues' panel**. This panel will be particularly helpful as a reminder if you are moving between sets of clues.

Once all four clues have been revealed, the button text changes to **'show answer'**.

Options bar:
The **sound FX** option allows you to turn off the sound effects that normally accompany correct and incorrect judgements.

Unchecking the **full screen** option will allow you to access other windows on the whiteboard.

The **exit** button closes the activity completely.

Don't Panic!

LEARNING OBJECTIVES

- Recalling prior knowledge;
- categorising musical words;
- developing knowledge and understanding of key musical terms.

DESCRIPTION OF ACTIVITY AND VARIANTS

Students compete in two teams to match musical words with the categories to which they belong. There are 5 variants of this activity, each with its own set of categories and a bank of musical words to match with them:

1. Musical elements   (7 categories / 42 words)
2. Musical instruments   (5 categories / 50 words)
3. Musical genres   (6 categories / 36 words)
4. Classic rock & pop hits   (7 categories / 42 words)
5. Numbers in music   (8 categories / 40 words)

WAYS OF USING THE ACTIVITY

Don't Panic! can be used to develop and consolidate students' knowledge and understanding of key concepts and vocabulary in an entertaining yet quite intensive manner. As with some of the other activities in this book, an educated guess can often result in new learning taking place.

The activity takes the form of a competition between two students, who could work unaided or as team representatives. A stimulus word or phrase is shown near the top of the screen. The aim is to be the first one to identify which of several categories it belongs to, by hitting the appropriate button. Stimulus words are generated in random order and without repetition. This means that a particular variant can be used several times over for revision/consolidation purposes without it becoming predictable.

Each student works from their own side of the board, with their own set of buttons. Once the stimulus appears, the students race to pick the correct category as quickly as possible. Only the first hit will be recognised.* If their answer is correct, a point is added to that student's score. However, if their answer is incorrect, then the opposing student has just a few seconds on their own to give an answer. If this too is wrong, the turn passes back to the first student, and so on.

If running *Don't Panic!* as a team activity, you may wish to decide whether or not conferring is allowed. If the students are permitted to take advice from their teams, the activity becomes far more interactive for the majority of students but also, of necessity, far more animated. If you prefer the quieter option, then students could be called up to the IWB in turn by you or nominated by their teams; in this case, you may need to agree how many questions each will attempt before passing on to another.

[* See cautionary note regarding pen-operated boards on the next page.]

Don't Panic!

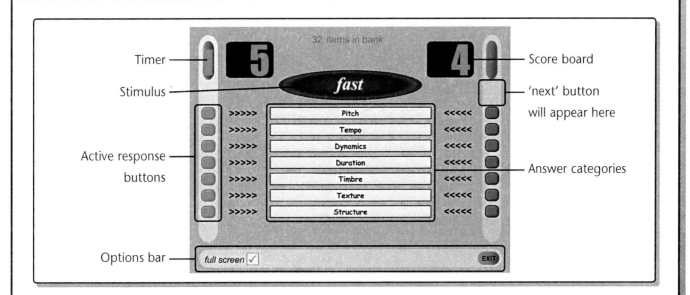

THE ACTIVITY SCREENS

Introductory screens:
These give operational guidance: *"This activity is for two competing teams, each with a volunteer standing on one side of the IWB. A musical word appears near the top of the screen. It belongs to one of the categories in the list below it. A point is awarded to the first team to identify the correct category. But if the first guess is wrong, the turn passes to the opposing team. If they also guess wrongly, or run out of time, the turn passes back to the first team again, and so on. Which team can score the most points?"*

Main screens:
The *'next' button* brings up a new random stimulus. *Response buttons* are used to choose the *answer category*; they are only active when coloured bright green. During this, the *timer* is frozen. If the answer is correct, a mark will be added to the *score board* for that student.

Options bar:
Unchecking the *full screen* option will allow you to access other windows on the whiteboard. The *exit* button closes the activity completely.

NB: Pen-operated IWBs will require two pens to play in this way. However, please note that some IWBs will be confused by simultaneous use of two pens and not respond as expected. If this is the case, you could run the activity as follows: the two students/teams raise their hands, call out or use some other agreed response to the stimulus; you decide which one produced an answer first and hit the appropriate button on their behalf; this way, only one pen is required and the IWB will function as normal.

QUESTIONS (STIMULI) AND ANSWERS (CATEGORIES) FOR ALL VARIANTS OF *PREDICT-ABILITY* CAN BE FOUND ON PAGE 25.

Blob Grid

LEARNING OBJECTIVES

- Performing a range of short rhythmic patterns;
- keeping in time with a beat;
- reading rhythms from notation (graphic and staff).

DESCRIPTION OF ACTIVITY AND VARIANTS

Students must perform short rhythms by sight from a symmetrical grid. There are 5 variants:

1. 4 x 4 grid   (simple metre, basic)
2. 4 x 4 grid   (simple metre, extended)
3. 5 x 5 grid   (simple metre)
4. 4 x 4 grid   (compound metre)
5. 4 x 4 grid   (graphic symbols)

Variants 1-4 each employ a different number of beats and/or a different metre, and can toggle between blobs and gaps and notes and rests. The rhythmic patterns could be clapped or played. Variant 5 uses up to four different graphic symbols and gaps in each pattern, which offers the opportunity for students to read them using 'body percussion' or different instruments. There is considerable progression both within and across the five variants. There is also an option for you or your students to create a new set of patterns.

WAYS OF USING THE ACTIVITY

There are a number of ways in which the grids can be read. For example, in a 4 x 4 grid:

- Select any one line/row and ask the class to perform it once or repeatedly.
- Ask the whole class to read the four lines one after the other, from top to bottom.
- Divide the class into four groups. Ask each group to perform one of the four lines/rows repeatedly (as an ostinato). The groups could enter in turn, at your signal.
- Again in four groups, each group is asked to perform all four lines in turn, but now entering one after the other (as a round). They start again at the top when the end of the bottom line is reached.
- When performing several parts at the same time, the use of different types of unpitched percussion (one timbre per part) will make the varied textures much clearer.

For variants 1-4, all of this can be done using either blobs or standard notation (via the 'standard notation' check box in the options bar), thus supporting the learning of note durations and rhythms. Be prepared to help students keep their place by pointing along the lines as they clap/play, especially when they are performing several lines in succession.

Just when the novelty of this might be wearing off, you now have the option of rotating the grid through 90° (in either direction), thus producing a new set of rhythms. This can be done several times, creating up to four sets of rhythms in all.

Blob Grid

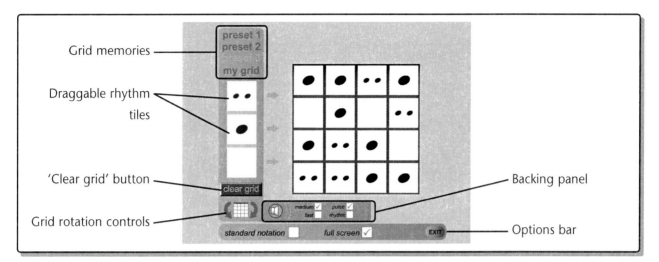

Grid memories

Draggable rhythm tiles

'Clear grid' button

Grid rotation controls

Backing panel

Options bar

You also have the option of providing the class with either a pulse or a backing rhythm at one of two given tempi, both to support them in keeping time and to add further energy to the activity. However, you may prefer to provide your own rhythmic support or have none at all.

Using the option to create a grid of their own, particularly in standard notation mode, can develop students' understanding of metre, note duration and bar construction.

THE ACTIVITY SCREENS

Introductory screens:
These give operational guidance: *"This version lets you see and build rhythm patterns in a (e.g.) 4 x 4 grid. You can view them as blobs or as standard music notation. The three presets cannot be replaced, but you can make temporary changes by dragging rhythm tiles from the toolbar to the grid. If you want to make your own pattern, be sure to click 'my grid' before you start dragging rhythms. Grids can be rotated with the tool at the bottom of the toolbar. This program is not designed to play the rhythms – that's down to you – but there are backing tracks."* Variant 5 (Graphic symbols) has minor textual differences in its guidance.

Main screens:
To use any of the three preset patterns, select one from the *grid memories*. To create a new pattern, click the *'clear grid' button* and drag *rhythm tiles* from the tool bar onto the grid. To move between 'blob' notation and standard notation in variants 1-4, change the option in the *options bar* at the bottom of the screen.

To produce a further set of patterns instantly, rotate the grid in either direction using the *grid rotation controls*. Note that, in its initial position, the grid has a darker shaded edge at the top, which can also be seen on the mini-grid between the rotation buttons. As the grid is rotated, this dark edge will give a clear reminder of the current orientation.

If a backing pulse or rhythm is required, open (and close) the *backing panel* by clicking on the 'backing' tab. Here you can choose between a medium or fast pulse/rhythm and start/stop it by clicking the speaker button. Click 'exit' to leave the activity.

THE RANGE OF PRESET GRID LAYOUTS AVAILABLE IS SHOWN ON PAGE 28.

Flash Card Rhythms

LEARNING OBJECTIVES

- Performing a range of short rhythmic patterns on sight;
- keeping in time with a beat;
- reading rhythms from staff notation.

DESCRIPTION OF ACTIVITY AND VARIANTS

Students must perform short rhythmic patterns by sight from a series of flash cards selected by one person. There are 5 variants:

1. 4/4 time   2. 3/4 time   3. 5/4 time   4. 6/8 time   5. Graphic symbols

The activity is similar to *Blob Grid* in its aims, but very different in the way it is run. It is also the only activity written in PowerPoint rather than Flash. Each of the five variants has twelve different rhythm patterns with a range of difficulty and so progression is available within each variant. Most of the patterns are single bars, with a few two-bar patterns in Variant 4. Since the flash cards can be selected in any order and left in view for any length of time, there can be a fast pace to the activity and the degree of challenge is in the hands of the person changing the flash cards. Backing rhythms are available to increase pace and motivation further.

WAYS OF USING THE ACTIVITY

You will first need to decide whether to use one of the backing rhythms provided or give a rhythm/pulse of your own, perhaps with a keyboard or percussion instrument.

Variants 1-4: these offer a single rhythmic backing pattern at two different tempi – you can change tempo or stop the backing at any point.* For example, you could start at the slower tempo and move to the faster one as students' confidence increases.

To start the activity, one person selects from the bank of rhythms the pattern that they wish the class to perform. Clicking on the pattern will open an enlarged flash card which the class must clap or play repeatedly until another appears. Clicking it again will take you back to the pattern bank, and the class should continue repeating the pattern until the next is chosen.

It is likely that students will have differing levels of confidence and experience in reading rhythms in staff notation; so having the class repeat each rhythm until it is secure will help them to associate sound and symbol and to develop confidence.

Of course you may prefer to use the activity to assess individual students' reading ability, in which case you can differentiate in your choice of pattern and increase challenge accordingly.

Variant 5: this has scope for the use of body percussion or vocal sounds, as it uses up to four different graphic symbols in each 4-beat pattern. You can decide beforehand what each symbol might mean, though a suggested key is provided on the screen. Since the challenge lies in performing a sequence of movements or sounds rather than actual rhythms, a wider range of backing rhythms and tempi has been provided for this variant.

[* See note on next page regarding backing rhythms in PowerPoint.]

Flash Card Rhythms

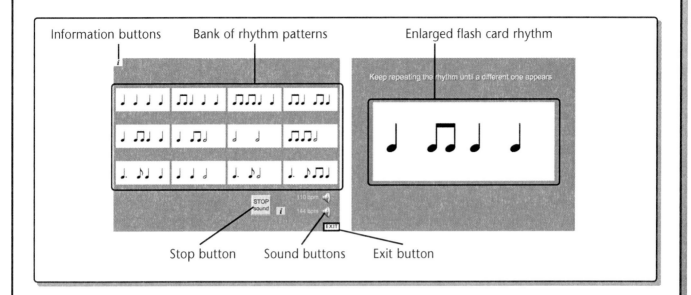

THE ACTIVITY SCREENS

Introductory screens:

These give operational guidance: *"In this activity, you must clap a sequence of (e.g.) one-bar rhythms in 4/4 time. One person chooses a rhythm for the class to clap. The class then repeats that rhythm until it is changed. Two different tempi are available for the backing."* Variant 5 (Graphic symbols) has minor textual differences in its guidance.

Main screens:

(The screenshots above apply to variants 1-4, but variant 5 works on the same principles even if some of the buttons look different.)

Click either of the *sound buttons* to start a backing rhythm. You can move between rhythms if you wish or stop a rhythm by clicking the *stop button*.

When clicked, the pattern selected from the *bank of rhythm patterns* will appear in a new screen as an *enlarged flash card rhythm*. Clicking on this will return you to the bank of patterns.

The *information buttons* will provide guidance if required.

The *exit* button closes the activity completely.

NB: The backing rhythm patterns are 'looped' within each variant. Since PowerPoint is not designed specifically as a music programme, there may be a very slight unevenness in the backing rhythms at the end of the first loop. This should rectify itself immediately and cause no further fluctuation in pulse thereafter.

**COPIES OF PATTERNS FOR ALL FLASH CARD VARIANTS
CAN BE FOUND ON PAGE 30.**

Mix and Match ~ Answers

Mix and Match 1: Symphony orchestra

Extract A: Off-beat snare drum
Xylophone on melody line
Trombone glissando

Extract B: Gentle, lilting drone rhythm
Low flute melody
Soft dynamics throughout

Extract C: Begins with brass fanfare
Ends with high, sweet violin melody
Repeated bass drone note through 2nd half

Mix & Match 2: String quartet

Extract A: DESCRIPTION 4
A legato violin melody against a repeated two-note (short-long) accompaniment in lower strings.

Extract B: DESCRIPTION 2
Begins with a 'conversation' between upper and lower instruments and ends with all together in unison. All instruments play pizzicato.

Extract C: DESCRIPTION 1
A slow legato violin melody played against a repeated drone note in the bass line.

Extract D: DESCRIPTION 3
Begins with two unison phrases, then an agitated violin tune against tremolo viola and off-beat pizzicato cello notes.

Mix & Match 3: Orchestral effects

Extract A: Smooth, deep bass notes throughout
Staccato (short) repeated violin notes towards end
Repeating pairs of detached notes on wind instruments

Extract B: Pizzicato (plucked) bass notes in second half
Rhythm has patterns of nine beats (4 + 5)
Staccato (short) violin notes at first, then smoother

Extract C: Starts and ends with a ff (very loud) note from all instruments
Features tambourine and timpani
Very high glissando (sliding) notes on violins in middle

Mix and Match ~ Answers

Mix & Match 4: Various styles

Extract A: Jewish Klezmer music
9 quick beats in a bar (2+3+2+2)
Violin plays 9-note ostinato pattern
Features accordion solo
Backing uses tambourine, drum, bass clarinet and double bass

Extract B: South American 'classical' music
7 quick beats in a bar (2+2+3)
Uses gong, claves and two pitched drums
Bassoon plays 7-note ostinato
Features tuba solo

Extract C: European 'classical' music
5 quick beats in a bar (3+2 and 2+3)
Features cellos on melody first
Double basses play occasional soft pizzicato notes throughout
Flutes and other high woodwinds take over melody half-way through

Extract D: Cuban jazz
Complex/uncertain metre
Uses bongos, congas, guiro and other Latin American percussion
Features saxes and trumpets in unison
Piano plays backing chords, with a brief 'fill-in' solo near the end

Mix & Match 2: String quartet

Extract A: Guitar riff as opening solo and then as part of backing
Features conga drums and drum kit
Soft sustained synthesizer sounds
Male vocal solo, with male and female backing vocals
Music comes from Africa (Zimbabwe)

Extract B: Talking drum solo begins the extract
Slow bass riff, repeated at two different pitches
Guitar backing moves with bass line
Male vocalist, no backing voices
Music comes from Africa (Mali)

Extract C: Opens with slow melody on reed-pipe instrument (sheng)
Features several high-pitched percussion instruments
Solo instrument (pipa) plucked with fingernails; several tremolo effects
All instrumental, but no bass sounds at all
Music comes from China

Extract D: Uses 'edgy' sound of dhol drum and bass sound of dhad drum
Bhangra fusion style
Instrumental links include rhythmic shouting
Male vocalist sings verse in Punjabi
Music comes from India

Predict-ability: Level 1

	Clue 1	Clue 2	Clue 3	Clue 4	Answer
Q1	Person	Composer born in 20th century	Specialises in film music	Wrote scores for the Star Wars films	JOHN WILLIAMS
Q2	Instrument	Made of metal	Played with a mouthpiece	Has 'valves' to help change notes	TRUMPET
Q3	Type of music	Popular style since 1970s	Started by New York disco MCs	Features DJing and rapping	HIP-HOP
Q4	Musical term	One of the 'elements' of music	Can be demonstrated by clapping	Patterns of different length notes	RHYTHM
Q5	Pot luck	A famous pop group	Consisted of four men	Started in 1960s Liverpool	BEATLES
Q6	Person	Austrian composer	Lived for just 35 years (1756-1791)	Child prodigy	MOZART
Q7	Instrument	Has strings	Plucked or strummed	Electric or acoustic	GUITAR
Q8	Type of music	Developed and changed over centuries	Traditional, passed on by ear	Sung by ordinary people	FOLK SONG
Q9	Musical term	Italian word	A dynamic	Abbreviated to 'f' in written music	FORTE
Q10	Pot luck	Electronic device	Fits in your pocket	Plays compressed audio files	MP3 PLAYER

Predict-ability: Level 2

	Clue 1	Clue 2	Clue 3	Clue 4	Answer
					Predict-ability: Level 2
Q1	Person	Male singer	Career spanned 40+ years from 1960s	Opera superstar (tenor)	PAVAROTTI
Q2	Instrument	Percussion	Usually has a skin	Has jingles around the rim	TAMBOURINE
Q3	Type of music	Started in Italy around 1600	Involves singers and orchestra	A play that is sung and acted in costume	OPERA
Q4	Musical term	One of the musical elements	Melodies need it, but rhythms don't	High and low	PITCH
Q5	Pot luck	Popular classical composition	Descriptive pieces by Frenchman Saint-Saëns	Includes *The Elephant* and *The Tortoise*	CARNIVAL OF THE ANIMALS
Q6	Person	German composer (1770-1827)	Composed Ode to Joy music (EU Anthem)	Kept composing despite deafness	BEETHOVEN
Q7	Instrument	Has strings	Played with a bow or plucked	Highest in orchestral string section	VIOLIN
Q8	Type of music	Started in New Orleans, early 1920s	Features blue notes, improvisation, syncopation	Varieties: Dixieland, Bebop, Swing, Trad, etc	JAZZ
Q9	Musical term	A dynamic	Italian for 'quiet'	Also common name for an instrument	PIANO
Q10	Pot luck	A country	Music includes classical raga, bhangra, Bollywood	Classical instruments include sitar, sarangi, tabla, dhol	INDIA

Predict-ability: Level 3

	Predict-ability: Level 3				
	Clue 1	Clue 2	Clue 3	Clue 4	Answer
Q1	Person	Male singer	Ex boy band member	Angels, Escapology, Intensive Care	ROBBIE WILLIAMS
Q2	Instrument	Made of metal	Used in jazz and pop, and sometimes classical	Mouthpiece has a single reed	SAXOPHONE
Q3	Type of music	Used for dancing	Stage music	Swan Lake, Nutcracker	BALLET
Q4	Musical term	Device used in composing	Melodic or rhythmic	Short repeated pattern	OSTINATO
Q5	Pot luck	Famous rock musician	Real name Paul David Hewson	Irish anti-poverty campaigner	BONO
Q6	Person	English composer	Portrait on £20 note	*Pomp & Circumstance, Land of Hope and Glory*	ELGAR
Q7	Instrument	Indian	Many strings	Ravi Shankar, George Harrison (Beatles)	SITAR
Q8	Type of music	Pop style	Bob Marley famous for this music	From West Indies (esp. Jamaica)	REGGAE
Q9	Musical term	Device used in composing	Bagpipes play this	Sustained or repeated note under music	DRONE
Q10	Pot luck	Famous song	Set to tune of *Londonderry Air*	Unofficial Irish anthem	DANNY BOY

Predict-ability: Level 4

		Clue 1	Clue 2	Clue 3	Clue 4	Answer
		Clue 1	**Clue 2**	**Clue 3**	**Clue 4**	**Answer**
Q1	Person	Multi-talented black musician	30 Top Ten hits - 24 Grammies since 1963	*Superstition, Sir Duke, My Cherie Amour*	STEVIE WONDER
Q2	Instrument	Hand drum	Range of sounds made by different strokes	African	DJEMBE
Q3	Type of music	Evolved in United States	Developed from African slave songs	Usually has 12-bar structure	BLUES
Q4	Musical term	Section found in most pieces of music	Sometimes slower than other sections	Starts the piece off	INTRODUCTION
Q5	Pot luck	Annual event since 1970s	Rock festival	Held in England (West country)	GLASTONBURY
Q6	Person	British rock star	Died of AIDS in 1991	Former lead singer with Queen	FREDDIE MERCURY
Q7	Instrument	Actually a set of several instruments	All percussion, one player	Rhythmic foundation of pop/rock bands	DRUM KIT
Q8	Type of music	Classical music genre	Normally 3 movements	Features solo instrument(s) and orchestra	CONCERTO
Q9	Musical term	Pop music term	Heard several times in a pop song	Catchy phrase to 'grab' the listener	HOOK
Q10	Pot luck	Note name	Black on the piano keyboard	Between F and G	F SHARP (or G FLAT)

Predict-ability: Level 5

Predict-ability: Level 5					
	Clue 1	**Clue 2**	**Clue 3**	**Clue 4**	**Answer**
Q1	Person	US swing band leader (and trombonist)	Went missing in 1942	In the Mood, Moonlight Serenade	GLENN MILLER
Q2	Instrument	Orchestral percussion	Usually played in sets (2, 3 or 4)	Also called 'kettle drums'	TIMPANI
Q3	Type of music	Classical music genre	Orchestral, usually 4 movements	Pastoral, Eroica, New World, Surprise	SYMPHONY
Q4	Musical term	One of the elements of music	How sounds are combined	Concerns layers of sound	TEXTURE
Q5	Pot luck	Rock anthem	Queen, 1975	'Mama, just killed a man...'	BOHEMIAN RHAPSODY
Q6	Person	Composer	19th century Russian	1812 Overture, Nutcracker, Swan Lake	TCHAIKOVSKY
Q7	Instrument	Tuned percussion	Metal bars	Name means 'bell-play' in German	GLOCKENSPIEL
Q8	Type of music	Serves a particular purpose	Needs to be gentle and calming	Sung to babies to send them to sleep	LULLABY
Q9	Musical term	Describes a particular structure	First section returns after middle section	A - B - A	TERNARY
Q10	Pot luck	Date in history and musical title	Famous Russian overture	Tchaikovsky included cannon and bells	1812

Don't Panic! ~ Answers

Don't Panic! 1: Musical Elements					
Key words (answers)	**Stimuli (questions)**				
Pitch	high	low	F sharp	B flat	treble	bass
Tempo	fast	slow	allegro	andante	rit.	accel.
Dynamics	loud	quiet	p	f	crescendo	diminuendo
Duration	long	short	crotchet	quaver	tie	dotted
Timbre	metallic	wooden	mellow	reedy	warm	tinkling
Texture	thick	thin	contrapuntal	multi-layered	solo	chordal
Structure	verse & chorus	ABA	rondo	call & response	variations	repeats

Don't Panic! 2: Musical Instruments					
Key words (answers)	**Stimuli (questions)**				
Woodwind	flute	piccolo	oboe	cor anglais	clarinet	bassoon
Brass	trumpet	trombone	French horn	tuba	euphonium	flugel horn
Stringed	violin	viola	cello	double bass	guitar	mandolin
Percussion	timpani	snare drum	tambourine	triangle	cabasa	claves
Keyboards	piano	harpsichord	accordion	synthesiser	organ	harmonium

Don't Panic! ~ Answers

Don't Panic! 3: Musical Genres						
Key words (answers)	Stimuli (questions)					
20th Century 'Classical'	Stravinsky	Britten	Pavarotti	Bernstein	Prokofiev	John Williams
Pre-20th Century 'Classical'	Mozart	Beethoven	Tchaikovsky	Bach	Baroque	Vivaldi
Jazz	Duke Ellington	Louis Armstrong	Be-Bop	Jools Holland	Jamie Cullum	Big Band
British rock and pop	Oasis	Iron Maiden	Stereophonics	The Beatles	Eric Clapton	David Bowie
American rock and pop	Elvis Presley	Jimi Hendrix	Madonna	Christina Aguilera	Michael Jackson	Kiss
World music	Raga	Gamelan	WOMAD	Steel Band	Didgeridoo	Samba

Don't Panic! 4: Classic rock & pop hits						
Key words (answers)	Stimuli (questions)					
Elvis Presley	Blue Suede Shoes	Don't Be Cruel	Hound Dog	Love Me Tender	Jailhouse Rock	All Shook Up
The Beatles	She Loves You	Yesterday	Yellow Submarine	A Hard Day's Night	Penny Lane	When I'm 64
Queen	Bohemian Rhapsody	We Are The Champions	We Will Rock You	Radio Ga Ga	Killer Queen	I Want To Break Free
Madonna	Hung Up	Sorry	American Pie	Vogue	Cherish	Like A Prayer
Elton John	Candle In The Wind	Rocket Man	Your Song	Circle Of Life	Pinball Wizard	Crocodile Rock
Michael Jackson	Billie Jean	Thriller	Beat It	Black Or White	Bad	Say Say Say
Abba	Waterloo	Dancing Queen	Super Trouper	Money Money Money	SOS	Mamma Mia

Don't Panic! ~ Answers

Don't Panic! 5: Numbers in music						
Key words (answers)	Stimuli (questions)					
More than six	*drum hits to begin EastEnders?*	*letters used to name notes?*	*pedals on a harp?*	*children of J.S. Bach?*	*strings on a mandolin?*	*symphonies by Mozart?*
Six	*"geese a-laying" at Christmas?*	*players in a brass sextet?*	*strings on a Spanish guitar?*	*finger-holes in a tin whistle?*		
Five	*"gold rings" for Christmas?*	*lines make a standard music stave?*	*notes in a pentatonic scale?*	*players in a wind quintet?*		
Four	*"Seasons" composed by Vivaldi?*	*singers in a barbershop quartet?*	*hands in a piano duet?*	*tenors in Il Divo?*	*quavers in a minim?*	*strings on a viola?*
Three	*"Steps to Heaven"?*	*sections in ternary form?*	*valves on a trumpet?*	*beats in a waltz bar?*		
Two	*notes in a cuckoo call?*	*bongos in a set?*	*Pet Shop Boys?*	*cymbals in a hi-hat?*	*violins in a string quartet?*	
One	*pitches in a monotone?*	*pitches in a unison?*	*leaders in an orchestra?*	*reeds on a clarinet?*	*operas by Beethoven?*	
None	*strings on a Jew's Harp?*	*instruments in an 'a capella' song?*	*notes in a rest?*	*trebles in a girls' choir?*	*black notes in C major?*	

Blob Grid ~ Preset Grids

Variant 1: 4 x 4 (simple metre, basic)

Preset 1 Preset 2 Preset 3

Variant 2: 4 x 4 (simple metre, extended)

Preset 1 Preset 2 Preset 3

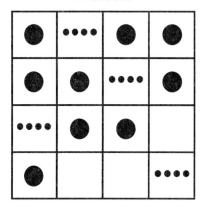

Variant 3: 5 x 5 (simple metre)

Preset 1 Preset 2 Preset 3

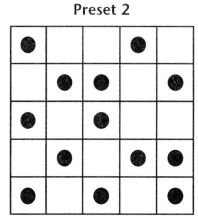
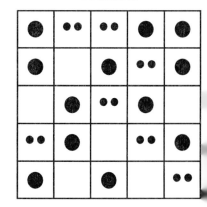

Blob Grid ~ Preset Grids

Variant 4: 4 x 4 (compound metre)

Preset 1	Preset 2	Preset 3
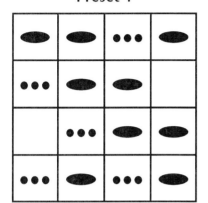	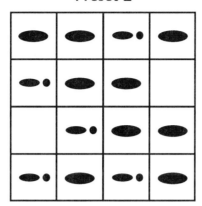	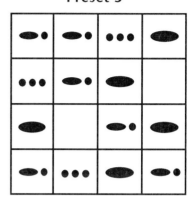

Variant 5: 4 x 4 (graphic symbols)

Preset 1	Preset 2	Preset 3
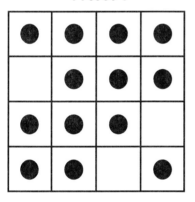	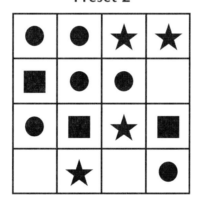	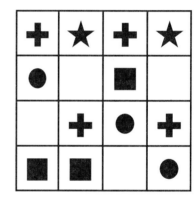

Flash Card Rhythms ~ Contents of Pattern Banks

Variant 1: 4/4 time

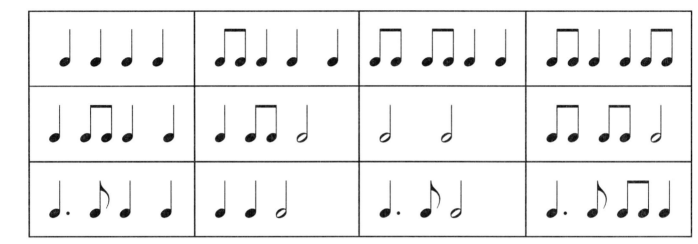

Variant 2: 3/4 time

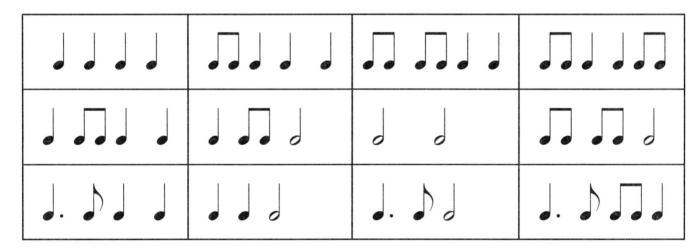

Variant 3: 5/4 time

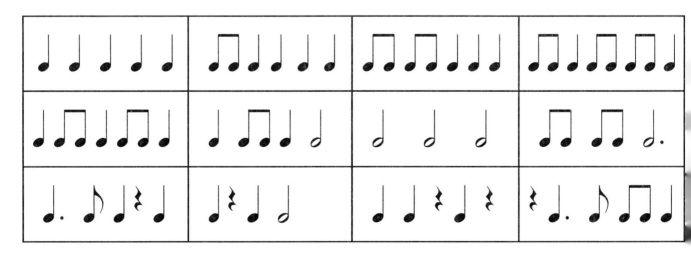

Variant 4: 6/8 time

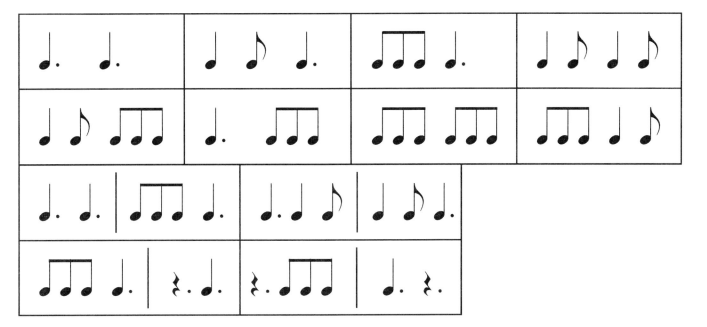

Variant 5: Graphic symbols

★ ★ ● ★	★ ● ★ ●	● ● ● ★	● ● ★ ★
★ ★ ✚ ●	★ ✚ ● ★	✚ ● ★ ●	✚ ✚ ● ★
★ ✚ ■ ●	✚ ■ ● ★	● ★ ■ ✚	✚ ■ ★ ●

APPENDICES 1

Frequently Asked Questions (Windows)

Will this CD-ROM work on all Windows systems?

It has been tested successfully on Windows XP. It may work on other Windows systems too but it is not designed for use with Windows 98. These menu and help pages have been optimised to work on Microsoft's own Internet Explorer browser, which is supplied with every Windows system. They may not work as intended if any other browser is used.

Does this CD-ROM need any special installation procedure?

No, the CD-ROM itself does not need to be installed and it will probably run automatically when you insert the disc. It is possible that, once only, you will be invited to install an Active-X control for Flash. This happens automatically if needed and you should accept the installation. See your network manager if the system reports that you do not have the necessary installation privileges.

If the program doesn't launch automatically when you insert the disc, go to the 'Start' menu, click 'Run' and type in D://index.htm (where D is the letter of the drive containing the disc), then click 'OK'. Or, on most systems you can just use the explorer to see the contents of the disc and double-click index.htm from the list.

Do I need to have any other programs installed?

Most of the CD will work without needing any other programs. The 5 Flash Card Rhythm activities will only run if Microsoft PowerPoint is installed on the same computer. This is one of the Microsoft Office suite of programs that are installed on nearly every school computer. (You also need a web browser to view these help and menu screens, but you do not need to be connected to the internet.)

Can I use any make of Interactive Whiteboard?

Yes. The activities do not rely on the additional facilities of any particular make of IWB. These facilities can still be used if desired, but they are not needed.

Will the activities run on a computer without an Interactive Whiteboard?

Yes. As the activities do not rely on particular IWB facilities, they can be run on a stand-alone computer using the mouse to interact with the information on screen. This also makes them suitable for use with data projector systems.

Can I run the activities from a hard drive?

Yes. Although this is not necessary, the activities will probably start with a little less delay if you copy them onto a hard drive. Remember that you are only allowed to copy the activities for use within your own school. Here's what to do:

- Decide where on your system you want to store the activities and create a new folder there.
- Rename the new folder as BadgerMusic, or whatever you like.
- Copy the entire content of the CD-ROM inside the new folder you have just created.
- Right-click the file index.htm inside the new folder and choose Send to > Desktop (create shortcut) from the pop-up menus.
- Rename the new desktop shortcut as BadgerMusic, or whatever you like.
- In future you can double-click the desktop shortcut to launch the activities without needing to insert the CD-ROM.

Can I run the activities from a laptop?

Yes, but remember that the built-in loudspeakers on most laptops are not suitable for class music listening. We recommend that you you use a laptop in conjunction with an external speaker system that gives a suitable volume level and bass frequency response.

Why don't the Flash Card Rhythm activities work on my system?

Please see Do I need to have any other programs installed?

Why do the backing rhythms stop after I select a new Flash Card Rhythm?

This problem has only been reported when using the Edirol UA-20 USB audio interface. It is only likely to affect the Flash Card Rhythm activities (PowerPoint files). You can probably cure the problem by always plugging in the USB connection after the computer has been powered up instead of leaving it connected all the time.

APPENDICES 2

Frequently Asked Questions (Mac)

Will this CD-ROM work on all Mac systems?
This CD-ROM has been tested successfully on OSX 10.3.9 and higher. We do not recommend its use on earlier systems. These menu and help pages have been optimised to work on Apple's own Safari browser (version 1.3.2), which is supplied with every Mac system. These pages may not work entirely as intended if any other browser is used.

Does this CD-ROM need a special installation procedure?
No, the CD-ROM itself does not need to be installed - just launch index.htm to get started.

Do I need to have any other programs installed?
Most of the CD-ROM will work without needing any other programs. The 5 Flash Card Rhythm activities will only run if Microsoft PowerPoint is installed on the same computer. This is one of the Microsoft Office suite of programs that are installed on many school computers. (You also need a web browser to view these help and menu screens, but you do not need to be connected to the internet.)

Can I use any make of Interactive Whiteboard?
Yes. The activities do not rely on the additional facilities of any particular make of IWB. These facilities can still be used if desired, but they are not needed.

Will the activities run on a computer without an Interactive Whiteboard?
Yes. As the activities do not rely on particular IWB facilities, they can be run on a stand-alone computer using the mouse to interact with the information on screen. This also makes them suitable for use with data projector systems.

Can I run the activities from my computer's hard drive?
Yes. Although this is not necessary, the activities will probably start with a little less delay if you copy them onto a hard drive. Remember that you are only allowed to copy the activities for use within your own school. Just copy the entire contents of the CD-ROM to a custom folder on your hard drive and launch the file index.htm from that directory to begin using.

Can I run the activities from a laptop?
Yes, but the built-in loudspeakers on most laptops are not suitable for class music listening. We recommend that you you use a laptop in conjunction with an external speaker system that gives a suitable volume level and bass frequency response.

Why don't the Flash Card Rhythm activities work on my system?
Please see Do I need to have any other programs installed?

Why doesn't the 'Close this window' link work?
In Safari 1.3.2, which was used during development of this CD-ROM, the 'Close this window' link will not work after any of the other internal links on this page have been followed. It only works if it is the first link that is clicked. The obvious work around is to close the window manually using the standard button in the top left corner of the frame. Maybe a future version of Safari might restore expected behaviour to the 'Close this window' link.

Badger Publishing Limited
15 Wedgwood Gate
Pin Green Industrial Estate
Stevenage, Hertfordshire SG1 4SU
Telephone: 01438 356907
Fax: 01438 747015
www.badger-publishing.co.uk
enquiries@badger-publishing.co.uk

Badger IAW Activities
KS3 Music Teacher Book and CD-ROM

First published 2006
ISBN 1 84424 816 X

Acknowledgements
Saxophone, Cello, Violin, Trombone, Tuba, Djembe and French Horn Audio files from 'Sound
clips' © Northumberland NGfL Virtual Orchestra
(http://ngfl.northumberland.gov.uk/music/orchestra/).

The organ sample (00'10") is taken from the start of Vincent Lübeck's "Preambulum in C",
from a Baroque Music Club recording: "An introduction to Baroque Organ Music" (BMC 3).
The harpsichord sample (00'10") is taken from the start of J.S. Bach's "Partita 2 in C minor"
(BWV 826) from a Baroque Music Club recording: "Bach's Harpsichord Partitas" (BACH 704).
You can find details at: http://www.baroquecds.com/03Web.html .

Harpsichord image from 'Images' © Michael Boys/CORBIS. Other images courtesy of iStock
Royalty Free Collection (www.istockphoto.com).

Publisher: David Jamieson
Editor: Paul Martin
Designer: Adam Wilmott
Illustrator: Adam Wilmott

Printed in the UK